LION IN THE STREETS

LION IN THE STREETS

Judith Thompson

Coach House Press Toronto

This play is dedicated to the children in Seaton Village, my neighbourhood in Toronto.

I would like to thank Gregor, Michael Ondaatje, Urjo Kareda, Bob Wallace, all the actors named in the cast lists, both Sarahs, and Francesca, who held and rocked three-week-old Grace while I transformed the hour-long radio play called 'A Big White Light' into *Lion in the Streets*. And, of course, Isobel.

Cover painting courtesy Urjo Kareda.

Great North Artists Management, Inc.
350 Dupont Street
Toronto, Canada
M5R IV9

The punctuation of this play carefully adheres to the author's instructions.

Published with the assistance of the Canada Council, the Ontario Arts Council, and the Ontario Ministry of Culture and Communications.

Canadian Cataloguing in Publication Data

Thompson, Judith, 1954-
    Lion in the streets

ISBN 0-88910-444-1

I. Title.

PS8589.H65L5 1992   C812'.54   C92-093319-X
PR9199.3.T56L5 1992

CONTENTS

INTRODUCTION

The Fractured Subject of Judith Thompson

During the extended six-week workshop in the Spring of 1990 that transformed Judith Thompson's radio play 'A Big White Light' into the first stage version of *Lion in the Streets* at the duMaurier World Stage Theatre Festival in June 1990, Judith Thompson the director would occasionally ask the stage manager, Nancy Dryden, to break the company and dim the light in the small back space at Toronto's Tarragon Theatre where the workshop was being held. While actors and others drank coffee and ran lines in the lobby, Judith Thompson the writer walked about alone in the darkened room, getting into the blood, as she says, of her characters. By the time the break was over she would present, with astonishing rapidity, new, remarkable, and quite unexpected passages of text, often replacing brilliant lines or even whole scenes that, however effective in themselves, were deemed to be expendable. Great lines, she says, are a dime a dozen.

Quite apart from her alacrity in cutting, Judith Thompson's process as a writer is consistent with her background as a graduate in English from Queen's University and from the acting program of the National Theatre School, and congruent with Tarragon Theatre's reputation as the home of poetic naturalism. Her own training as an actor no doubt reinforced Thompson's well-developed sense of characterization and her acute ear for dialogue; and Tarragon Theatre has proven for almost a decade a congenial host for Thompson's writer-in-residency and a valued first producer for all but her first play.

But if poetic naturalism, however evocative, were all she wrote, Judith Thompson would not have the reputation she does as the creator of disturbing and dislocating theatrical experiences. *Lion in the Streets*, like all her plays, betrays an abiding interest in psychological motivation, and evokes immediate empathy for characters who are conceived in depth. Unlike those in more conventionally naturalistic plays, however, the characters in *Lion in the Streets* tend to be fragmented and discontinuous, and they are rarely contained within a single, unified action or linear plot. They tend, too, to be represented self-consciously as constructs undergoing crises of subjectivity, struggling to bridge a persistent gulf between the self that speaks and the self represented in that discourse as the subject, the 'I.' As the characters struggle to construct a *unified* self through a narrative that will allow them to understand—or 'comprehend'—their lives, the play's plot becomes the site of duelling, contradictory, and even mutually exclusive narratives— multiple actions that are disturbingly open and exploratory rather than comfortably closed. This seems to be the case on the level of character and individual scene, in which the often violent or disjunctive actions are matched by a radical uncertainty about what is 'really happening,' about whose point of view is 'true,' and under what circumstances. But it is also the case that the overall 'relay' structure of the play resists closure, containment, and easy comprehension, as a character from each scene is carried forward to the next, catalyst to a new action. As Thompson said, during a panel discussion at the duMaurier World Stage, 'I just couldn't cope with the idea of a huge body of narrative.... I started to find that kind of narrative tedious, because your expectations are usually fulfilled.' Replacing the unity of traditional linear narrative are the overarching but problematic presence of Isobel, the play's collage-like composite portrait of an urban neighbourhood in crisis and, in production, a multiplicity of associative visual and musical linking devices such as the act-ending dances and the evocative disk that featured above centre-stage in the original duMaurier World Stage and Tarragon productions.

Naturalistic drama traditionally relies on the creation of fully empathetic characters whose psychological crises—constructed by the plays as personal neuroses—precipitate conflicts in the action. These conflicts are resolved through a 'reversal' in the play's central and linear plot, producing in the central character(s) a 'recognition' of an already existing, 'well-adjusted,' and unified 'self' whose problems have been explained as deviations from a hegemonic social 'norm.' The empathy created between character and audience in such plays in turn produces a cathartic release of potentially disruptive emotions in an audience that leaves the theatre satisfied—calm of mind, all passion spent. Such plays, then, serve to *contain* potential social and psychological unrest, to explain disturbances and dissatisfactions in terms of individual psychology, and by purging discontent to affirm the social and political status quo.

In the plays of Judith Thompson, and most clearly in *Lion in the Streets*, intense empathy with naturalistically conceived character functions quite differently: in spite of a presentation of character that is psychologically acute, nothing is explained *away*. As she remarked at the duMaurier World Stage panel session, 'I don't want to write industrial plays that play to psychology classes.' Thompson's characters experience a conflict between a self that is submissive to the inherited and hegemonic discursive practices of society and a self that is not synonymous with the subject of that discourse. The conflicts in *Lion in the Streets*, far from moving towards resolutions that leave characters and audiences satisfied that things must be as they are, present occasions for potential—and potentially redemptive—transformation. The audience is not allowed to settle comfortably into a single, consistent, or unified way of viewing or empathizing with the characters, to identify actor with character, to feel superior awareness to the characters, or to construct any but provisional narratives with which to contain and comprehend the action. And to the extent that the play invokes closure, it does so without authority; that is, it invites the audience to *make* sense, to take responsibility for the meanings and for the world that its members individually construct from their *own* distinct subject positions. At the conclusion of *Lion in the Streets*, the apotheosis of Isobel is nevertheless redemptive, not as a logical, natural, or inevitable outcome of the play's actions, but as an active exercise of will—or even faith—on the part of an audience that is urged to 'take your life. I want you all to have your life.'

Lion in the Streets is a profoundly disruptive, socially subversive, and deeply religious play. It revisions traditionally phallo- and logo-centric structures and languages, perverts the linearity of Aristotelian reversal and recognition, and replaces these with more radically contingent and consciously constructed shaping devices. And as in much feminist drama (as pointed out by Hélène Keyssar in her book, *Feminist Theatre*), the inevitability of reversal becomes in this play the possibility of transformation; recognition (of an already existing, unified subject) becomes the conscious selection of a subject position that is useful and meaningful in a particular context, and that allows audience members similar selection; and the experience of catharsis becomes the more unsettling but less enervating experience of fragmentation. Using the tools and intensity of psychological realism, *Lion in the Streets* dramatizes crises of subjectivity, and because its characters are characterized as constructs and presented as subjects in continuous process of construction, those crises are presented as providing for the possibility of change.

In spite of its realistic scenes of harrowing brutality and of ruthless emotional and intellectual honesty, the fracturing of subjectivity and revisioning of dramatic structure in *Lion in the Streets* are consistently used to insinuate the possibility of choosing and achieving 'grace.' And while the playwright sees 'truth' as a passive state of tension, something that 'happens to you through not doing anything,' she posits 'grace' in her unorthodox theology as the product of active human *will*, including the wills of audiences: 'Truth,' she says in an interview with Judith Rudakoff in *Fair Play*, 'is simply what *is* …. Grace is something you achieve. Through work. And Grace is something you have to work and work at. It happens through penitence, through sight. Through seeing who you are and changing things.'

Richard Paul Knowles, March 1992

LION IN THE STREETS

Lion in the Streets was first produced as the inaugural Public Workshop Project at Tarragon Theatre in Toronto in May 1990, with the following cast:

ISOBEL, Tracy Wright
NELLIE, LAURA, ELAINE, CHRISTINE, SHERRY, Jane Spidell
RACHEL, LILY, RHONDA, ELLEN, SCARLETT, Ann Holloway
SCALATO, TIMMY, GEORGE, DAVID, RODNEY, BEN, Stephen Ouimette
MARTIN, ISOBEL'S FATHER, RON, FATHER HAYES, MICHAEL,
    Andrew Gillies
SUE, JILL, JOANNE, BECCA, JOAN, Maggie Huculak

Stage Manager: Nancy Dryden
Workshop Assistants: Urjo Kareda, Richard Paul Knowles,
    Andy McKim
Set and Costume Design: Sue LePage
Music: Bill Thompson

Lion in the Streets received its world premiere at the duMaurier Theatre Centre as part of the duMaurier World Stage Theatre Festival in Toronto in June 1990, with the same cast.

Director: Judith Thompson
Set and Costume Design: Sue LePage
Sound Effects: Evan Turner
Lighting Design: Steven Hawkins
Stage Manager: Nancy Dryden
Production Assistants: Urjo Kareda, Richard Paul Knowles,
    Andy McKim
Production Manager: Martin Zwicker
Set Construction: George Vasiliou
Wardrobe: Cheryl Mills
Properties: Mary Spyrakis
Apprentice A.S.M.: Henry Bertrand

Lion in the Streets subsequently was remounted with a revised text by Tarragon Theatre in Toronto in November 1990, with the following cast:

ISOBEL, Tracy Wright
NELLIE, LAURA, CHRISTINE, SHERRY, Jane Spidell
RACHEL, LILY, RHONDA, ELLEN, SCARLETT, Ann Holloway
MARTIN, ISOBEL'S FATHER, GEORGE, MARIA, DAVID, MAN,
    RODNEY, BEN, Robert Persichini
SCALATO, TIMMY, BILL, RON, FATHER HAYES, MICHAEL,
    EDWARD, Julian Richings
SUE, JILL, JOANNE, Clare Coulter

Director: Judith Thompson
Set and Costume Design: Sue LePage
Lighting Design: Steven Hawkins
Composer and Performer: Bill Thompson
Sound Design: Evan Turner
Stage Manager: Nancy Dryden
Apprentice A.S.M. and Dance Captain: Nancy Katsof
Electrician: Patrick Hales
Sound Operator: John Alderman
Set Construction: George Vasiliou and Will Sutton
Scenic Painting: Gabriele Schnutgen and David Rayfield
Properties: Kate Hemblen
Wardrobe: Cheryl Mills and Sue Ward
Assistant Lighting Design: Paul Mathiesen
Waltz Coach: Viv Moore

This published text includes sections rewritten since the Tarragon premiere.

Tracy Wright (ISOBEL) and Clare Coulter (SUE) in the
Tarragon production, November 1990

ACT I

The ghost of ISOBEL, *a deranged and very ragged looking nine-year-old Portuguese girl, runs around and around a large circle, to music, terrified of a remembered pursuer, in fact, the man who killed her in this playground seventeen years before the action of the play. There are autumn leaves all over the playground, and the kids who approach her all have large handfuls of leaves, which they throw at her. At this point* ISOBEL *does not know she is a ghost, but she knows that something is terribly wrong. She is terrified*

ISOBEL Doan be scare. Doan be scare. [*turns to audience*] Doan be scare of this pickshur! This pickshur is niiiice, nice! I looove this pickshur, this pickshur is mine! [*gesturing behind her*] Is my house, is my street, is my park, is my people! You know me, you know me very hard! I live next house to you, with my brother and sisters, Maria, Luig, Carla and Romeo we play, we play with your girl, your boy, you know me, you know me very hard. But … when did tha be? Tha not be now! Tha not be today! I think tha be very long years ago I think I be old. I think I be very old. Is my house but is not my house is my street but is not my street my people is gone I am lost. I am lost. I AM LOOOOOOOOOST‼

[*Four children—two girls and two boys—laugh and approach* ISOBEL]

NELLIE Take a bird why doncha?

RACHEL Go back with the nutties to the nuttyhouse!

SCALATO She looks like a crazy dog!

MARTIN [*barks*] Hey!

[*All bark*]

ISOBEL Peoples! Peoples, little boy little girl peoples! Hey!

[ISOBEL *walks towards them*]

MARTIN What's she doin?

NELLIE She's coming over here!

RACHEL She's gonna get us!

ISOBEL You, girl, you help to me. I am lost you see! You help!

NELLIE She smells.

RACHEL You should dial 911 so the police could help you.

SCALATO Where do you live?

MARTIN With all the other pork and cheese west of Christie Street?

RACHEL Martin that's not nice.

ISOBEL [*overlapping*] Portuguese, Portuguese, yes ... I catch a bus! Is there a bus, bus maybe? To take me to my home? You know a bus?

SCALATO No buses here.

ISOBEL Yah, bus right here, bus right here, number ten, eleven, I take with my mother to cleaning job, where this bus?

SCALATO I said there's no buses here you ugly little SNOT.

ISOBEL [*points*] You! YOU bad boy you bad boy say Isobel, BAD.

SCALATO Why don't you get your ugly little face outa here, snot?

MARTIN Snotface!

ISOBEL Shut up boy, shut up, I kill you I kill you boy.

SCALATO Hey she's gonna kill me!

RACHEL She's a witch.

[ISOBEL *tosses rocks at them*]

MARTIN She's throwin rocks! Hey she's throwin rocks!

NELLIE STOP IT.

RACHEL Stop throwin rocks or we'll tell the police!

ISOBEL You BAD boy you BAD I will kill you!

SCALATO [*jumping off, attacking her*] You just try it you goddamned faggot!! Faggot! Faggot!! [*hitting her*]

ISOBEL [*growling like a dog*] G-r-r-r-r-r. G-r-r-r-r-r.

[*They circle one another*]

MARTIN What's she doing?

NELLIE I don't like her.

[ISOBEL *and* SCALATO *scrap and the others join in.* SUE, *a thirty-eight-year-old woman in a grey sweatsuit, walking home from a meeting, spies the fight and rushes up*]

SUE Hey! Hey hey hey stop that right now!

[SUE *pries them apart*]

HEY! Listen! What is going on??

ISOBEL I KILL YOU BOY!

SCALATO She started it!

MARTIN She was throwing rocks at us!

ROSE She's crazy.

[ISOBEL *leaps towards* SCALATO. SUE *catches her, she falls to the ground*]

SUE Little girl? Little girl!

ISOBEL [*overlapping*] I kill that stupid boy.

SCALATO She started it, lady.

MARTIN I'm getting out of here.

SCALATO Me too.

NELLIE & ROSE Wait for me!!

SCALATO You chicken, Martin! You suck!

ISOBEL I kill that stupid boy! [*beat*] I no like those boys.

SUE I'm sorry if they hurt you.

ISOBEL They no want play with me. Why they no want play with me? Why all the kids no want play with Isobel? Ha?

SUE Ohhh ... sometimes kids are just ... mean, that way, Isobel, when I was little kids were mean like that to me once.

ISOBEL Kids? Mean no play to you?

SUE That's right. We had just moved to a new town, Cornwall actually, near Montreal? Well my sisters and I went for a walk around the neighbourhood and these big boys on bikes started firing arrows at us.

ISOBEL Boys on bikes?

SUE That's right, just like those nasty boys!

ISOBEL Nasty boys, to you, too! Mean to you!!

SUE That's right. And those arrows, they hurt! They really hurt!!

And I was the oldest so I told my sisters, 'Just cry, just start to cry and then maybe they'll feel sorry for us,' so we all started to cry.

ISOBEL Cry.

SUE But you know what? It didn't work! They kept shooting those arrows anyways. They were just *mean*.

ISOBEL Mean boys shoot arrows. Haaah!

SUE AND suddenly, a bigger boy, about sixteen, came along and made them stop, and you know, he was like an angel, to us, an angel who came down from the sky on his big blue bicycle I've never forgotten that.

ISOBEL Never forgetting.

SUE Nope. I guess I'm your helper today.

ISOBEL Helper.

ISOBEL'S FATHER [on porch] Hey! Is-o-bel.

SUE Isobel is that your father?

ISOBEL Father. My father. Eu pensava que té tinha perdedo!

ISOBEL'S FATHER [ordering ISOBEL to go around to the back door] Vai pela porta das traseiras.

SUE Hello.

[ISOBEL'S FATHER grunts]

My name is Sue Winters and I don't know if you're aware of it, but some of the boys in the neighbourhood have been well I'd say doing some not very nice teasing of your daughter. I just … thought … you might …

[He goes in, slamming the door]

Poor man probably works all day in construction and then all night as a janitor in some Bay Street office building. What a life.

[SUE exits]

ISOBEL My father? My father is not there. My father is dead. Yes, was killed by a subway many many years; it it breathed very hard push push over my father; push over to God. Hi my father.

[Music. Lights come up just a bit. SUE is in her son TIMMY's room, in the dark. TIMMY is in bed. ISOBEL watches]

SUE And so the giant starfish saved the drowning boy.

TIMMY What was the starfish's name?

SUE The starfish's name? Uh ... Joey. It was Joey.

TIMMY Mummy? Why isn't magic true? I want magic to be true.

SUE Well. It is true, in a way, it ...

TIMMY Not it's not. It's not true. And ya know what else?

SUE What, darling?

TIMMY I think tonight's the night.

SUE That what, Tim?

TIMMY That we're all gonna die. Tonight's the night we're gonna die.

[*Music. A dinner party, around a table.* ISOBEL *is there, invisible. The conversation is simultaneous*]

LAURA There was nothing to do! Nothing to bloody do but sing in the church choir!! And go to baked-bean suppers!! The snow at one point was actually up to the second-floor window.

BILL No, she had the *gall* to ask my male students to, 'Please leave the room,' for her senior seminar. She did 'not wish to be dominated by men.' Where did that leave me, I asked her?

LILY No, no no, you have to pat the dough, pat it for ohh a good five minutes then put it in the microwave for one, then take it out, then pat it again.

GEORGE St. Paul said, 'We are as vapour,' what is it? Like 'vapour vanisheth' or—something. 'We are no more.' So I got up this notion of Martians—being these—wisps of vapour ... No, you see your problem is you want the aliens to be like you, you are anthropomorphizing, you ...

LAURA That's so boring. That's so knee-jerk boring.

BILL And she launched into the most savage tirade—

[SUE *rushes in, dressed in her sweatsuit and sneakers. Everyone turns and freezes, except* BILL, *who continues to talk until* SUE's *third 'Bill'*]

SUE Bill ... Bill ... Bill!! We have to talk!

BILL Sue! Hi! Who's with the boys?

SUE Mum came over, Bill I need to talk, NOW.

LAURA Would you like a drink, Sue? We have ...

GEORGE Yeah, come in and sit down ...

Maggie Huculak (SUE) and Andrew Gillies (BILL) in the
duMaurier production, June 1990

SUE No, no thank you, I just ... want to talk to my husband.
ISOBEL My helper, Suuuuusan!
BILL Oh—okay, Sue, I'll just finish this conversation. Anyway—
SUE He thinks he's going to die.
BILL Who?
SUE Timmy! Your son! He—
BILL What, did he say that tonight? Oh, that's just kids, he's—
SUE BILL, come home, your son is very depressed his father is never
    there, why are you never never ...
BILL Sue PLEASE, we'll talk about it later, okay? So as I was saying,
    Laura ...
SUE Come with me.
BILL I'll come in a while. I'll just finish this conversation, and then
    I'll come, okay?
SUE YOU COME WITH ME NOW!
BILL Sue.
SUE Bill, I need you, please, why won't you come?

BILL Why won't I come? Why won't I come? Because ...

[BILL *walks over to the others*]

I'm ... not ... I am not coming home tonight.

SUE Bill! Stop it, this is private—

BILL It is not private, Sue, nothing we do is private for Christ's sake, you tell your friends everything, they all—know—everything— about us, don't they? How many times we had sex in the last month.

LAURA I don't think that's true, Bill.

GEORGE I haven't heard anything.

SUE Bill, I think you're being very unreasonable.

[*There is an awkward pause in which* BILL *and* SUE *lock eyes*]

LAURA [*to* LILY *and* GEORGE] Well, it's a lovely night out there. Why don't the three of us go for a walk?

BILL No.

SUE You stay and finish up that wonderful looking chocolate paté, Laura, I'm sure you spent a lot of time on it. I'll just get Bill's coat and we'll go on home.

BILL There is ... somebody else, Sue. And I will be going home with her.

GEORGE I think we've all had a little too much to drink, why don't we just ...

SUE Don't worry guys this isn't real. He's just drunk he's just trying to scare me because we had this argument about the new sofa— Come on honey, let's go home. Who is it. Who is it, Bill? She's not here, is she? You didn't, you didn't bring her to my neighbours', OUR friends' dinner party, to which I was invited. Laura! Laura for God's sake.

LILY It's me.

[SUE *laughs*]

LILY Why do you think I'm joking?

SUE [*looks at* LILY, *looks at* BILL] Bill??

BILL This is—Lily.

LILY How do you do, Susan?

SUE Don't you call me by my name you FAT!! Please, I don't think you know what you're doing. This is not just me, this is a family, a family, we have two children.

LILY I'm sorry.

SUE Bill you are not leaving your children.

BILL Sue, please.

SUE YOU TOOK A VOW! In a CHURCH in front of a priest and my mother and your mother and your father and you swore to LOVE and honour and cherish till DEATH US DO PART till DEATH US DO PART BILL, it's your WORD your WORD.

BILL I am breaking my word.

SUE No!

BILL YOU turned your back on me!! You you—look at you in that ... sweatsuit thing you're not—I mean look at her, really, you're you're you're a kind of ... cartoon now, a ... cartoon mum a ... with your day-care meetings and neighbourhood fairs, you know what I mean Laura! Your face is a drawing your body, lines. The only time, the only time you are alive, electric again is ... when you talk on the phone, to the other mums, there's a flush in your face, excitement, something rushing through your body, you laugh, loudly, you make all those wonderful female noises, you cry, your voice, like ... music, or in the park, with Timmy and John, while they cavort with the other children at the drinking fountain, spraying the water and you talking and talking with all the mothers, storming, storming together your words like crazy swallows, swooping and pivots and ... landing ... softly on a branch, a husband, one of us husbands walk in and it's like walking into ... a large group of ...

LILY You see, I love ... his body, Sue. I mean, I really love it. I love to suck it. I love to kiss it his body is my God, okay? His body—

[SUE *slaps* LILY *twice*]

SUE YOU ... DON'T LIVE ON THIS STREET. You don't belong in this neighbourhood.

[LILY *contains herself from slapping* SUE *back*]

Where did you meet this ... woman? On the street?

[BILL *starts to try to answer*]

In a house of prostitution? I demand to know—

LILY I fucked him on the telephone, Susan, many many times.

SUE That is a disgusting ... lie.

LILY Come on Suzy, don't you remember? You caught him a couple of times, on the downstairs phone with his pyjamas around his ankles, he told me!

SUE [*the wind totally out of her*] I thought he was making ... obscene phone calls.

BILL Hello.

LILY Hi there.

BILL You got back to me quickly.

LILY Fucking right.

BILL Fucking right.

LILY Your voice makes me crazy.

BILL My voice.

LILY I'm wet, Bill, wet just from hearing your voice.

BILL What are you wearing?

LILY Black silk underwear, red spiked heels, black lace bra.

BILL Yeah? And what do you want? What do you want?

LILY I want to suck your big cock, Bill, would you like me to do that? Would you like me to suck your big cock?

BILL Oh baby, baby.

LILY And then I want you to fuck me from behind all night long, can you do that? Can you do that for me, Bill?

BILL Yes, yes, oh yes! Yes! Yes!

LILY Oh, Bill!

SUE BILLLLLLLLLLLLLLLLLLLLLLL!!!!!!!

[SUE *physically attacks* LILY]

Aghhhh! Listen, you, if you take my husband away from me and my children I will ... kill you, I will I will ... come when you are sleeping and I will pull your filthy tongue out of your filthy mouth. And then I will ... feed it to our cat.

BILL Susan.

SUE [*forced laugh*] I didn't mean that, I really didn't. I'm sorry everybody, this is all just so ridiculous and embarrassing and I'm sure we'll all laugh about it someday I KNOW we will, but um ... Bill?

Won't you just ... give me a chance? To show you? That I can? Be sexy? Cause I can, you know, much much more so than THAT creepy shit ... Don't you remember? Don't you remember before we were married how you loved to watch me dance? Come on, you did! Remember remember that wedding, Kevin and Leslie's? I wore that peach silk that you loved so much that dress drove you crazy! And after after the wedding we were in that room in the Ramada Inn over the water and I danced? You lay on the bed and you just ... watched me you loved it I ... whooshed whooshed in that dress, back and forth to this thing on the radio back and oooh and back and you were laughing and and [*laughs*] and whoosh.

[*Music beats louder, filling the room, and* SUE *begins a slow striptease*]

And whoosh ... and ... close to you, you're hard ... and far away and ... turn ... and whooosh ... and ... let ... my ... hair ... down ... you—love my hair whoosh and ... zipppper ... whoooo down so slowwwww turn and turn ... you watching lying on the bed and ease ... off my shoulders you love my shoulders, elegant ohhh Billy, and down. Over my body the soft silky down and whoooooooooooooooo whooOOOOOOOOO Billy. Take me home, Billy, take me home and let's make mad passionate love! Please.

[BILL *and* LILY *leave.* GEORGE *and* LAURA *pick up* SUE*'s clothing and bring it to her.* LAURA *dresses her*]

LAURA Honey, I'm sorry.

SUE Aghh don't feel sorry for me it's fine, everything will be fine because ... his colon cancer's gonna come back, don't you think? Dr. Neville said he had a sixty-forty chance, it will. And she'll drop him, for sure, don't you think? And he will let me nurse him I will ... feed him broth, with a spoon, like I did my mum, and I will hold, I will hold his sweet head in my chest till till his lips are black and his eyes ... like bright dead stars and he is dead and I will stay I will stay with his body, in the hospital room because I did love that body ... oh I did *love—that—body* once.

ISOBEL Susan, Susan, Susan. The boy with the arrow ha *killed* you, ha? Where's your helper now? Oh Susan, you can't help me now you can't take me home. [*to the audience*] Hey! Who gonna take me home? You? You gotta car? What kinda car you got? Trans-Am? What about bus tickets? You gotta bus tickets? C'mon. Come on. COME ON. SOMEBODY. What I'm sposed to do, ha? Who gonna take me home? Who gonna take me home?

[ISOBEL *finds a watching place. A few hours later, at* LAURA *and* GEORGE *'s,* LAURA *clears the table*]

LAURA Poor Suzy. Poor poor Suzy.

GEORGE [*half asleep*] Yeahh. Chee.

LAURA God, that is the worst thing I have ever seen happen to anybody.

[GEORGE *and* LAURA *laugh hysterically and imitate* SUE *in the previous scene*]

GEORGE Whoosh! That peach silk, oh baby take me home.

LAURA Take me home, Bill. Let's make mad passionate love. [*stops imitating* SUE] I don't know, I mean I know she needs a friend badly, I am her friend I mean I love her. George, how can you laugh? This is important. If she calls me tomorrow, what should I say? I'm just going to say, I'm going to say, 'SUZY? I feel really badly for you and I think you're a wonderful person but you will have to look somewhere else for—'

GEORGE Nice.

LAURA GEORGE, you KNOW—

GEORGE You always say she's your best friend, Laura, 'my BEST'—

LAURA She is! But George, are you forgetting Maria? I had a nervous breakdown because of that woman and her problem how could you FORGET?

GEORGE I was on the book tour, Loo.

LAURA I told you about it a hundred times, how could you forget?

GEORGE I was on the book tour—Loo.

LAURA George, you are so insensitive, I can't believe this. I told you about it one hundred times. How can you forget?

[GEORGE *grabs a tablecloth and wraps it around his head, like a shawl, speaking in a Portuguese accent*]

GEORGE How could I forget, how could I forget?

LAURA George.

GEORGE Looka this. Me? I donta forget nothing.

LAURA George I'm going to bed, Molly gets up in two hours and it's always me that gets up with her of course.

[*She walks around the circle*]

GEORGE/MARIA LAURA.

[*Now he speaks as* MARIA, ISOBEL's *mother.* ISOBEL *recognizes her*]

LAURA George! Come to bed.

GEORGE/MARIA LAURA.

LAURA Maria.

MARIA I am ... so sorry to be coming to your house, maybe you busy, I don't know—

LAURA No, no, please come in Maria, I'm just—reading the paper the kids are at school and—

[MARIA *starts shaking violently and keening. She looks like she is in shock*]

Maria? ... uh ... Maria? Are you alright? You look—why don't you sit down. Here. Sit down. Can I get you a drink of water?

[MARIA *starts to keen with grief, quite quietly*]

MARIA Eeeeeeee

LAURA Maria? Maria ... are you alright? Maria, Maria please tell me ... what's ...

MARIA ... I think ... I think ... Antonio—

LAURA Your husband? Something happened to your husband?

[MARIA *continues to keen*]

It's okay, Maria, you don't have to tell me if you don't—

MARIA Five o'clock in the morning I cook: smelt and three scramble eggs, nice bread, coffee. For Antony must work long day, construction on highway, long day in the sun, he come from his shower to kitchen, but he don't want. He gotta rat in his stomach that day he say, make a joke, don't want my cooking eat a little bitta bread and just small glass of milk and he go, catch his subway.

I fold. I fold clothes one pile for Antony, one pile for me, one
for Maria, Romeo, ISOBEL and Luig, my hands fold the clothes
but my ... [*gesture indicating self or soul*]

LAURA Sure, you go on automatic—I—

MARIA Like I fold myself too, and I go in his body, maybe, you
know, his ... hand to, wipe off his face when he hot and too
sweat I am there;

[*She walks operatically down-stage and delivers the rest of the
speech, which should be like an aria*]

I am foldin a light sheet of blue then and sudden, I can see
through his eye, am at subway, in him, he stands on the plat-
form, is empty, empty and I am his head, circles and circles like
red birds flying around and around I am his throat, tight, cannot
breathe enough air in my body the floor the floor move, and
sink in, rise up rise like a wall like a killin wave turn turn me in
circles with teeth in circles and under and over I fall!

[ISOBEL *falls on an imaginary track in front of her mother*]

I fall on the silver track nobody move I hearing the sound. The
sound of the rats in the tunnel their breath like a basement these
dark rats running running towards me I am stone I am earth
cannot scream cannot move the rats tramp ... trample my body
flat-ten and every bone splinter like ...

[*We hear the sound of a strong wind as the 'Sugar Meeting' is being
set up on the stage. By the end of the wind,* LAURA *is at her table,
addressing the meeting*]

LAURA Good evening everybody.

GEORGE Good evening.

RON Hi Laura.

LAURA I uh might as well get straight down to business. As head and
sole member of the menu research committee, I have spent some
three weeks doing ... a great deal ... of ... research, and even a
little detective work ...

[RON *and* GEORGE *are talking to one another*]

... and I would like to make my presentation tonight without too much interruption, thank you.

GEORGE Go for it.

RON No problem.

LAURA POINT ONE. Sugar: I strongly recommend that we make a concerted effort to eradicate all sugar from the children's diet. Sugar is an overstimulant, sugar is empty calories, sugar rots ...

RON Uh, I have to say, that, while I agree, sure, too much sugar is not a good thing, that once in a while ...

LAURA Would you let your four-year-old smoke 'once in a while'?

[*A murmur from the crowd*]

RON [*with a little laugh*] I don't really think you can equate ...

[ISOBEL *rises and walks into the meeting*]

LAURA Sugar is a known carcinogen, Ron, I have a study right here ...

JILL Lettuce is a known carcinogen, for God's sake!

ISOBEL Hey! Boys! Girls! Looka this! I think tha they can't see me! They no see Isobel! Wha happen? Wha happen?

JILL Okay as chairperson, I say—let's cut the comments and raise our hands for questions. Laura? You want to go ahead?

LAURA Yes, thank you, Jill. Uh. [*clears throat*] It has come to my attention ...

[GEORGE *groans*]

Excuse me, I have to ask you why you groaned like that, George, did I say something wrong?

JILL George, penalty for groaning out of turn, just kidding.

GEORGE No, no, I'm sorry, I just, I don't know, I just ... have a kind of a hard time with 'meeting ... talk' ... 'it has come to my attention.'

LAURA Well, I'm very sorry, George, if you have a better way of—

JILL That was uncalled for George, really.

RON George, your mother's calling you.

[*General laughter*]

JILL Let's let Laura continue please, so we can get out of here ...

ISOBEL I think I invisible!

LAURA Thank you Jill. I have NOTICED, if you don't like 'it has come to my attention,' I have noticed that in this nursery school they are … subtly, and I'm sure unwittingly, encouraging an addiction to sugar in our children.

RHONDA Hey, that's not true.

LAURA Rhonda, I'm SAYING it's not intentional …

RHONDA The kids are not …

LAURA PLEASE LET ME TALK.

JILL Go ahead, Laura, please.

LAURA I have noticed that sugar is used as a reward. If you're good we'll make cookies tomorrow. If you tidy up you get chocolate cake as a reward. You are creating … unwittingly, I concede, you are creating TOMORROW'S COKE ADDICTS … TO—

RHONDA EXCUSE ME I HAVE TO SAY THAT, AS THE CAREGIVER, I RESENT THIS.

LAURA Rhonda, I'm not accusing just you, I think you are fabulous with the kids, it's our whole society …

RHONDA I am not creating drug addicts.

JILL Rhonda, Laura does not mean any of this personally, I think that's …

LAURA I'm saying it's a small step from sugar addiction to—

RON Excuse me, I have to say, all food is sugar …

LAURA REFINED SUGAR IS FAST-ACTING, RON, IT BURDENS THE PANCREAS.

GEORGE I think you are taking this a little too seriously, Laura, we're just talking about a few cookies now and then for heaven's sake.

LAURA WE ARE TALKING ABOUT A LIFETIME ADDICTION AND I DON'T THINK IT SHOULD BE TAKEN LIGHTLY.

JILL Laura, are you willing to listen to a response from Rhonda?

LAURA Sure.

RHONDA I would just … like to say that I, also have done … a great deal of studying diet and menu and that, and I fully agree with Laura that sugar is … something to be avoided, IF YOU CAN. Listen, if I'm giving the kids yoghurt, they won't eat it without honey they won't, so I figure, a bit of honey is worth getting the yoghurt down em …

LAURA BULLSHIT THAT IS ABSOLUTE UNADULTERATED
BULLSHIT.

RHONDA I beg your pardon, Laura?

LAURA You don't know what you're saying, Rhonda.

RHONDA If you don't trust me, Laura ...

LAURA Rhonda ...

RHONDA I do not encourage sugar, I do not hold it up as a reward,
ever, I have never done that.

LAURA You're lying, Rhonda.

RON WAIT A MINUTE HOLD ON JUST A ...

LAURA SHUT UP RON. LISTEN. LISTEN TO ME RHONDA. I
FOUND OUT THAT JUST LAST FRIDAY, LAST FRIDAY,
AS A REWARD, YOU TOOK SIX KIDS, INCLUDING MY
TWINS, TO A DOUGHNUT SHOP. YOU TOOK THEM
TO A DOUGHNUT SHOP AND BOUGHT THEM EACH
A JELLY DOUGHNUT. I think I screamed for five minutes
when the twins told me that I just couldn't believe it they started
harassing me every five minutes, 'Mum, if we're good, can we
have a jelly doughnut?' I don't think they'd ever HEARD
OF JELLY DOUGHNUTS BEFORE THAT!! I find it
unconscionable, UNCONSCIONABLE that a jelly doughnut
would be the sole purpose of an excursion.

RHONDA Um, I can explain that. It was a Friday, right, and I
happen to get severe cramps with my period, right? And I was
very sick that day and the kids had bad bad cabin fever, well ...

LAURA [overlapping] And the Friday before that it was popsicles,
Rhonda, I'm not blaming you I'm saying you need to be
re-educated, we all do, smelling the flowers is a reason to go for a
walk, not getting a poisonous body-destroying drug ...

RHONDA LET MEEEEE TALLLLLK. LET ME TALK LET ME
TALLLLLLLLLLLK!! I feel ... nailed to the wall by you lady,
nailed right to the fucking wall. I have to say and something else
I have to say is that I think you are ... are very ... inconsiderate
... of feelings! I brought up two kids on what I feed your kids,
and they turned out just fine, are you telling me what I feed my
kids isn't good enough for your kids? You know the funny thing
is, Laura, you may be a bitch on wheels, but lookin at all the

rest of you, Laura? at least you're honest you are. Youse others, what you're thinkin is ... it really doesn't matter what they get at the day care the real learning is at home, that's where youse teach your kids to become—huh. Here I am saying 'youse' I haven't said that since I was a kid! that's how flustered I am—at home you teach your kids ... to be ... higher kind of people, higher kind of people don't eat Kraft slices and tuna casserole, I've seen that kind a laugh in your voices, all of you, when you say, 'Oh, they had "tuna casserole,"' I seen, I have seen the roll in your eyes at the grace before meals, or the tidy-up song, or the stars we give out for citizen of the week, you think, oh well the kid is happy, well cared for, we can undo all that and we can make the kids high people like ourselves better people, more better people than the poor little teacher who reads ROMANCE, yes, yes, JILL MATHINS, I saw you showin my book, my novel to RON there and Cathy and havin a big giggle, you think I didn't see that? You think the books you read are deeper more ... higher, well it's the same story, don't you see that? What's makin me cry in my book is, when ya come right down to it, is exactly the same thing that's makin you cry in your book, oh yes, oh yes and I'll tell you something, I'll tell all of you I GREW UP ON THAT. I grew up on jelly doughnuts and butter tarts, and chocolate ice-cream, and I happen to think they're a wonderful thing. I happen to agree with the mice and the cock-roaches and the horses and birds that treats are a wonderful thing, you need treats, you need treats in this life, each bit of a treat can wipe out a nasty word, every bite of a jelly doughnut cleans out your soul it is a gift from GOD, a wonderful gift from GOD and I for one ... I for one ... I ... for ... your eyes, eh? Your eyes are all the same colour and shape like a picture, a ... freaky art picture all the same in a row like dark soldiers raisin your ...

[ISOBEL *shoots everybody there except* RHONDA *with her finger. There are real shot sounds although* ISOBEL *is imagining this*]

ISOBEL [*big laugh. Struts*] Rho-HONDA! Bebbe! Beautiful belle! I have killed those dirty bastards, babe, I have killed them dirty dead. I am your harmy, Rhohonda! And you! You gonna take me home!

[ISOBEL *falls and wraps herself around* RHONDA*'s feet. Music. A restaurant.* DAVID *takes his place behind the bar, another person is sitting alone at a table.* RHONDA *and her friend* JOANNE *meet for drinks. They are laughing.* ISOBEL *watches*]

RHONDA Oh man is this Singapore Sling fantastic.

JOANNE My Fuzzy Navel is warm. Hot!

RHONDA SEND it back! We're paying through the teeth for these drinks. Waiter, take this thing back!

JOANNE No, I like it this way, honest, Rhonda, I do.

DAVID Is there a problem with your cocktail?

JOANNE No no no no please ...

DAVID I could take it back —

JOANNE No.

RHONDA Are you sure?

JOANNE I'm sure.

DAVID Okaaay.

RHONDA Ohhh Christ, I'd like to just sit and drink all afternoon to tell you the truth.

JOANNE I thought you quit heavy drinkin.

RHONDA I did. I'm just ... down in the dumps.

JOANNE Why, ya on your time?

ISOBEL Is this my home? This is not my home!

RHONDA No no no, I get happy then, no, it's just ... work.

JOANNE Yeah, Jeez I'm glad I'm not workin it made me crazy, what's goin on? the kids at the day care gettin to ya?

RHONDA No no it's not the kids, the kids are great, it's the parents.

JOANNE Uh oh. That same B-I-T-C-H?

RHONDA No, she was quite good this time, strangely enough, it's another one.

JOANNE They all look like bitches to me in their leather pants. Stuck up, puttin their kids in forty-five-dollar shoes, I looked at the price of them REEboks for kids—the other day when I picked you up I saw three of those kids had those shoes on I couldn't believe my eyes.

RHONDA Yeah, well, they're pretty well-off, but I don't hold that against them, I mean, who wouldn't be if they had the chance, right?

JOANNE Well that's a good point SO ...

RHONDA We had this meeting, okay?

JOANNE RHONDA. Excuse me!

RHONDA What?

JOANNE [intake of breath] ... I don't know.

RHONDA What do you mean?

JOANNE I mean ... no, I don't know.

RHONDA Joanne.

JOANNE I mean ... Oh God, I wasn't going to tell nobody—

RHONDA You're pregnant again?

JOANNE No no no no, if only, I ...

RHONDA JOANNE, I'M YOUR BEST FRIEND.

JOANNE YOU'RE MY BEST FRIEND?

RHONDA Yes, you know that!

JOANNE THEN SWEAR ON YOUR MOTHER'S LIFE.

RHONDA What?

JOANNE That you will do what I'm gonna ask you.

RHONDA Joanne, what is this?

JOANNE Just ... swear.

RHONDA I'm not swearing on my mother's life without knowing what it is, she's got enough problems ...

JOANNE Okay, your husband's life.

RHONDA Okay, I swear on the asshole's life. There. Now what?

JOANNE You remember ... I had this pain in my back?

RHONDA Yeah, for the last few months, every time ya bend down.

JOANNE SEARING pain, every time I moved ...

RHONDA ... Okay ...

JOANNE Well remember I told you I went to that specialist and he said he was gonna do some tests?

RHONDA Right, uh-huh.

JOANNE Well—

RHONDA You gotta go in and have an operation and you want me to take your kids, no problem of COURSE I'll take them Jo, for God's—

JOANNE [overlapping] No. No, I mean, you might have to take the kids but that's only ... part of it.

RHONDA Joanne, I really don't like guessing games.

JOANNE Shadows ... that's what they call them, and ... it is ... the very worst thing it could be, and the ... kind, the kind is of the bone.

RHONDA Oh boy.

JOANNE Yeah.

RHONDA [whispers] Jo ...

JOANNE Don't ... don't touch me. I'll go hysterical please.

RHONDA YOU ... want a cigarette?

JOANNE Yeah.

[RHONDA *lights one and gives it to her*]

Ya know, I have to go to the bathroom, like, real bad but I'm not gonna go, ya know why? Cause every time ... I sit down to pee I feel my whole life drainin out of me, just draining out with the pee, goin ... outa me, into the water down in the pipes, and under the ... friggin ... GROUND. That's where I'll be, Rho, that's where I'm gonna ... [*fights to regain her composure*] I'll come home with the groceries? Like after dark? and I'll see Frank and the kids through the window, in the livin-room, right? Watchin TV, or drawing on paper, cuttin out stuff, whatever, and I'll stand on the porch and watch em, just ... playing ... on the floor, and I think ... that's life, that's life goin on without me, it'll be just like that, only I won't be here with the groceries, I'll be under the ground under the ground with my flesh fallin off a my face and I just can't take it. You know in that picture? That picture I had in my bedroom growing up?

RHONDA UHH—

JOANNE My aunt and uncle sent me that from England, the poster it's OPHELIA, from this play by Shakespeare, right? And she she—got all these flowers, tropical flowers, wild flowers, white roses, violets and buttercups, everything she loved and she kinda weaved them all together. Then she got the heaviest dress she could find ... you know how dresses in the olden days were so long and heavy, with petticoats and that? And she got this heavy heavy blue dress, real ... blue and then she wrapped all these pretty pretty flowers round and round her body, round her head, and her hair, she had this golden, wavy hair, long, and then she steps down the bank, and she lies, on her back, in the stream. She lies there, but the stream runs so fast she's on her back and she goes. It pulls her along so fast and she's lookin at the sky and the clouds, and she's singing little songs—'I'm lookin over a four-leaf clover'—and being pulled so fast by a clear cold water pulled along and she's not scared, she's not scared at all, she's calm, so happy! And just ever so slowly her dress, gets heavier, right? Then, then, she gets caught on a stick, like a branch, of a willow tree, and her dress pulls her down, soft, she's still singin down deep deep deep to the bottom of the stream and with all these 'fantastic garlands,' these beautiful flowers all around her— 'one's for the roses that blew down the lane'—she dies, Rhon, she dies ... good. She dies good.

RHONDA That's ... something.

JOANNE I want to die like that. But ... I don't ... want to do it all alone, I mean, I want you to help me, with the flowers, and with the dress, and my hair, I want you to make sure the willow branch is there, and the stream is right, and maybe ... maybe that ... Frank ... sees I ... wouldn't mind him seein ... me in that stream, with the flowers, and the heavy blue dress ... I wouldn't mind if you took maybe some pictures of me like that and then you could have them printed and given out at the funeral, something like that ... just, you know, two by four, colour, whatever, it's the one thing that would make it alright— it's the one thing ...

RHONDA I just ... I don't know, Jo, you know I'd do anything to make it alright ...

JOANNE Well this is what I want, Rhonda, it's really really really what I want. Are you going to help me?

RHONDA I uh—think you need to see a counsellor, Jo, you know they have counsellors that ... specialize in these ... situations I'm surprised your doctor didn't ...

JOANNE You think I'm crazy.

RHONDA No no, Joanne, I just think that ... your situation is so hard that you are not quite yourself, I mean this is not ... you, the Joanne I know is practical she ... you should believe in the treatments, Jo, they do work sometimes, they really do, and the

Joanne I know—would never ask a friend to help ... her ... is one of the most thoughtful people that I know, of other people and how the hell, how the hell do you think that I could live with that after, eh?? I mean it's all very lovely and that, your picture, in your room but that's a picture, that's a picture, you dimwit! The real of it would be awful, the stalks of the flowers would be chokin you, and the smells of them would make you sick, all those smells comin at you when you're feelin so sick to begin with, and the stream, well if you're talking about the Humber River or any stream in this country you're talkin filth, in the Humber River you're even talkin sewage, Jo, you're talkin cigarette packages and used condoms and old tampons floating by you're talking freezin, you'd start shakin from head to toe you're talkin rocks gashin your head you're talkin a bunch of longhairs and goofs on the banks yellin at you callin you whorebag sayin what they'd like to do to you, you're talkin ... and where would you get a dress like that, eh? You'd never find the one in the picture, Jo, it'd be too tight at the neck and the waist, it'd be a kind of material that itches your skin, even worse wet, drives you nut-crazy, the blue would be off, wouldn't look right your shoes wouldn't match you could never find the same colour, Joanne. You can't become a picture, do you know what I mean? I mean you can't ... BE ... a picture, okay?

[*They freeze.* ISOBEL *runs from her watching place, around the circle screaming; she has realized, listening to* JOANNE, *that she is not lost, but dead, murdered seventeen years before*]

ISOBEL AAHHHHHHHHHHHH!! I am dead! I have been bones for seventeen years, missing, missing, my face in the TV and news-papers, posters, everybody lookin for, nobody find, I am gone, I am dead, I AM DEADLY DEAD! Down! It was night, was a lion, roar!! with red eyes: he come closer [*silent scream*] come closer [*silent scream*] ROAR tear my throat out ROAR tear my eyes out ... ROAR I am kill! I am kill! I am no more!

[*Music*]

[*to* JOANNE] We are both pictures now. WHO WILL TAKE US?

WHO WILL TAKE US TO HEAVEN, HA?

[*Lights down. Cathedral bells ring.* DAVID *is outside, walking down the street*]

DAVID God, that customer dying of bone cancer. I didn't even want to touch her glass. I don't know she had that look, that dead look. I mean I almost felt hostile.

ISOBEL [*inside the cathedral*] I WANT TO GO TO HEAVEN NOW!

[*She sees a life-size statue of the Virgin Mary and approaches it*]

Holy Mary Mother of God. Will you take Isobel to heaven now, please?

[*She lies at the base of the statue, her hand touching the statue's foot*]

DAVID God that cathedral is beautiful, funny, I've passed it every day on my way out from work and I've never really looked at it. Look at the stonework, those *spires*—

[*He opens the church doors and enters. The doors slam behind him*]

Oh I love this it's so ... the air is so ... holy it IS, look at those bird-bath things full of holy water, I love it it's so primitive. [*he splashes some on his face*] In the name of the Father ... the Son, and the Holy—

FATHER HAYES Good evening.

[DAVID *shrieks, startled. His shriek echoes*]

It's alright, it's alright. Have you come for ...

DAVID Confession. I've come for confession, 8:30, yes? I'm not too late, am I, see, I just finished work, and ...

FATHER HAYES Not too late, of course not.

[FATHER HAYES *goes into his part of the confessional*]

DAVID [*to himself*] I guess just—God I don't remember a THING about what to do!!

[*We hear the wooden barrier being opened, and the priest begins the Latin prayer*]

FATHER HAYES In the name of the Father, and the Son, and the
    Holy Spirit.
DAVID [*overlapping*] Oh God he's saying something—
FATHER HAYES May the Lord be in your heart and help you to
    confess your sins with true sorrow. Let us listen to the Lord as he
    speaks to us: I will give them a new heart and put a new spirit
    within them; I will remove the strong heart from their bodies
    and replace it with a natural heart, so that they will live accord-
    ing to my statutes, and observe and carry out my ordinances;
    thus they shall be my people and I will be their God.
DAVID [*overlapping*] I think it's Latin, isn't that against Papal Law? I
    should report him to the Vatican and have him defrocked here
    goes nothing—

[FATHER HAYES *finishes the prayer*]

AHH—FORGIVE ME FATHER FOR I have sinned. It has
been … four weeks since my last confession. These are my sins?
… OKAY, told Barb I'd be there last night for dinner with her
and the niece and nephew—didn't show up didn't phone
nothing, was in a mad PASH with my hockey player. I was very
cruel to Daniel Thursday, saw him at Billy's—the club? And I
don't know, the way he was looking at me drove me CRAZY
CRAZY he was mooning! Well I walked up to him and told him
to 'quit mooning I'd rather see your hairy ass than that pathetic
face, face it!' I said, 'Face it you old fag, you have been dumped,
DUMPED!' That was really mean, that's gotta be more than a
venial sin, AND THEN, then, yesterday, I walked through a
park? And I saw a large group of poor children playing, and I
just thought they were trouble; I wondered why God had put
them in the world, really, isn't that unkind? THEN today I saw
a fat lady eating an ice-cream cone and I said, I think quite
audibly I said 'disgusting' oh AND I did not stand up in the
subway the incredibly packed subway, for a hugely pregnant lady
and her kid, I just didn't feel like it. Quite the catalogue, eh?
Oh and another thing, I've lied to you already. I haven't been to
confession in fifteen years, haven't stepped in a church in fifteen
years, just … did it on a whim, don't ask me why I was passing

by on my way ...

FATHER HAYES AND you felt the hand of GOD?

DAVID Well ... it was just a whim—really ...

FATHER HAYES David.

DAVID How do you know my name?

FATHER HAYES David I know your name better than I know my own.

DAVID Wait a minute, wait a minute, I think maybe this is some odd coincidence because although my name is DAVID, I don't actually know you at all, so ...

FATHER HAYES There's nothing odd about it, David, you were an altar boy for me, two years, for two years you served, in 1957 and 1958 at St. Bernard's in Moncton, New Brunswick. Remember?

DAVID Moncton? We were around there for a couple of years—

FATHER HAYES You were a believer, David, the other boys were just forced into it by their parents, you believed in every statue every—

DAVID Father Hayes? You—are Father Hayes?

FATHER HAYES I am.

DAVID You're still alive?

FATHER HAYES I think.

DAVID But you were so old even way back then!

FATHER HAYES Not really.

DAVID I remember you now. I remember you did look old, because you stooped, and you had white hair already didn't you?

FATHER HAYES Indeed, I was prematurely white ...

DAVID White hair and ... and ... red eyes.

FATHER HAYES I ... suffered from allergies, hay fever. I'm sorry if it frightened you.

DAVID I guess maybe it did frighten me a bit, Father, but you know how young boys are—

FATHER HAYES I am sorry, but, but ...

DAVID No no, I ... look, I uh—

FATHER HAYES David, I want ...

DAVID ... don't mean to be impolite but I'd like you to be honest with me, sort of man to man I ... I always got the impression that you were looking at me much more than you looked at the other boys am I right?

FATHER HAYES Well ...

DAVID I felt ... I felt as though your eyes were devouring me.

FATHER HAYES No, no, no ...

DAVID No?? I'm gay, Father, you can be honest with me. I'll forgive you, I mean you never actually did anything, you never even touched me, you just ... looked. You kept looking at me—tell me, tell me the truth.

FATHER HAYES It was not what you think, no, no please—

DAVID Confess to me Father, come on, come on ...

FATHER HAYES I make my confessions on a regular ...

DAVID Have you confessed this sin?

FATHER HAYES No, no I haven't, but—

DAVID God loves sinners who confess, Father, you taught me that, as long as you speak up and you're sorry as hell, you're okay, you still got your ticket to heaven, but you won't you won't Father, if you don't tell me, you'll wither in LIMBO! I suffered, I need you to tell me! CONFESS ...

FATHER HAYES I'm due to a christening. I have to shave first, there's a big party, I—

DAVID You would christen a baby with this sin, bobbing on the surface, bobbing? Confess, you son of a bitch. Con—

FATHER HAYES Forgive me Father for I have sinned.

DAVID Alright.

FATHER HAYES I looked at you, David, because ... I ... because ... I wanted ... to ... remember ... you.

DAVID Remember me?

FATHER HAYES Because ... of what was to happen, in the water: oh OH when the day arrived, when the picnic came round, in July, that Canada Day picnic? I had a bad feeling, I had ... a very bad feeling indeed. We all piled out of the cars: families, priests, nuns, altar boys, piled out and lugged all those picnic baskets to tables under trees. The grownups all fussed with food and drink while the kids, all of you children, ran ran in your white bare feet to the water, throwing stones and balls, and a warning sound a terrible, the sound of deep nausea filled my ears and I looked up and saw you, dancing on the water, and I saw a red circle, a red, almost electric circle, dazzling round and round like waves, spinning round your head and body. I thought watch, watch that boy, on this day he will surely drown, he *will*. David, *I knew that you would die*. And all because of the chicken. The twenty-nine-pound chicken brought there by Mrs. Henry grown on her brother's farm, everyone had talked and talked about that chicken, who would carve that chicken, Mrs. Henry took it out you skipped along the shore, she laid it on the table, 'FATHER HAYES, YOU GO AHEAD AND CARVE, AND DON'T MAKE A MESS OF IT OR YOU WON'T SEE ME AT MASS NEXT SUNDAY.' Everyone laughed laughed the men, the men drinking beer, watching me, sure they're thinking, 'Watch him carve like a woman,' most men hate priests, you know this is a fact, I could see them thinking cruel thoughts under hooded eyes and practised grins; my sin was the sin of pride! The sin of pride David, I started to carve, didn't want to look up, lest I wreck the bird. You see at that moment that chicken was worth more, indeed worth more ... than your LIFE, David I SHUT OUT the warning voice and I—carved. I carved and carved and ran into trouble, real trouble I remember thinking, 'Damn how does any person do it, it's a terrible job,' people behave as if it's nothing, but it's terrible, I kept at it, I wouldn't give up, I wouldn't look up till I'd finished, and I finished carving, and I had made a massacre. The men turned away the women ... murmured comfort, and before I looked up I had a hope, a hard hope, that you were still skipping on the rocks and shouting insults to your pals all hands reached for chicken and bread, potato salad, chocolate cake I looked I looked up and your hand from the sea, your hand, far away, was reaching, reaching for me far away ... oh no! I ran, and tripped, fell on my face ran again, I could not speak ran to the water and shouted as loud as I could but my voice was so tiny; I saw your hand, ran to the fisherman close, he wasn't home his fat daughter and I, in the skiff, not enough wind no wind, paddling paddling, you a small spot nothing then nothing the sun burns our faces our red red faces.

DAVID And I ... was ... never found?

FATHER HAYES And now ... you have come!! You have finally come!!

DAVID And what have I come for?

[FATHER HAYES *is sleeping*]

DAVID Uh ... Father? Uh—listen ... I'm sorry. I'm sorry but

Robert Persichini, Jane Spidell, Clare Coulter, Tracy Wright,
Ann Holloway and Julian Richings in the Tarragon production,
November 1990

I never died. You got the wrong guy I knew you ... some other
time—I mean, shit, I wish I had died, I only wish, it would have
made my life so much more interesting ... I grew up, I grew up.
Listen if I had drowned in the sea, in Moncton, New Brunswick a
beautiful perfect young boy, if I was ... pulled by the sea if I reached
and was lost, and all those people felt this loss, a loss all their lives,
mother father brothers and sister friends a dark ache, somewhere
in their chest for what could have been, they could all imagine, you
see, what could have been Father Father? I forgive you, I forgive
you Father, it was nice on the water, you know? It was neat, so
calm, as I slipped underneath I wasn't scared, I'll tell ya. I wasn't
scared a bit. The water was so ... nice!!

[*Music.* ISOBEL *dances, joined by the cast one by one until they are
all dancing fully. Cast dance off one by one leaving* ISOBEL, *who
freezes. Blackout*]

ACT II

Sounds of kids playing in a park, a group of mothers chat. ISOBEL *watches*

CHRISTINE How's your pregnancy going, dear?

[*Lion roar*]

ISOBEL I hear the LION, I hear the Lion ROAR!!

ELLEN Wonderful! I finally feel ... good for something. LEO, SHARE IT. Share it please.

CHRISTINE Not me NOT me when I was pregnant I felt as useful as a cow. A large, stupid ...

ELLEN Christine!!

CHRISTINE EMMA! Five more minutes honey! Mummy's got to go to work! Well, considering I despised the man whose child I was carrying—

ELLEN I suppose that would ... alter things— GOOD CATCH, Leo!

SUE Hi guys. Timmy, just five minutes. Remember, your father's coming to get you at five.

CHRISTINE Sue, I love that blouse! Really suits you!

ELLEN Gorgeous!

SUE Thank you, I'm organizing a bake sale, if you can believe it, for the community centre over on Ash Street. PLEASE say you'll bake, or sell tickets, even a promise to buy—

ISOBEL I must tell these peoples, I must tell them now!

ELLEN Forget me, I'm a diabetic! I can't even look at the stuff!

SUE Tim! Why don't you try the swing? You love swings.

CHRISTINE Okay, put me down for fudge brownies, *if* my kids don't eat them first.

[GEORGE *enters with a kid's bicycle*]

George! How's the book going?

GEORGE Well, well, very well indeed!! And how's the busiest freelancer in town? Bradley, don't push so hard!

CHRISTINE Overworked and underpaid.

GEORGE What else is new?

[RON *enters*]

Ron! Why aren't you at your office?

ELLEN We're telling!

GEORGE Good, Bradley!

SUE Tim? Why don't you try the swing?

CHRISTINE RON did you get my note? EMMA PUT IT BACK!

RON Yes, I did, I—I—I—

ISOBEL [*hitting them*] Shut up Boy! Shut up Girl! I say I say it's time!! He's in the streets get them out he's in the streets save your children take their hand take their leg.

SUE Isobel! I saw this girl before, she—

ISOBEL I say shut up! I say LISTEN TO ME NOW! Can you no hear? Listen! Can you nooo—

[*All freeze except* SUE, *who crosses slowly towards the children*]

SUE Timmy?

ISOBEL [*goes to her*] The lion is here, in your streets. He is trying to kill you, to kill all of your children. He really really is.

[*She picks up a great crooked stick which she will carry until she says 'I love you' to* BEN *in the final scene*]

Watch me! [*laughs*] I am your HARMY! [*laughs*] I am your SAINT! I am your HARMY! Watch me, watch me, [*a war cry*] I WILL KILL THE LION NOW!!

[*Thunderstorm as* SUE *shouts 'TIMMMYY!!' and the others ad lib to their children, e.g., 'Quick, you don't want to get wet!' All exit. A kid's bike is left on-stage. Blackout. Lights up on* CHRISTINE *walking towards* SCARLETT*'s basement apartment, 'tracked' by* ISOBEL]

ISOBEL This girl, Christine, Christine, this girl, SHE will take me to the lion, yes, for she ... she is very hard. Harrrd. HARRRRRRRD!!

CHRISTINE 116 Carlisle. Lord what a stench. What could that be? [knocks]

SCARLETT Come in!

CHRISTINE Scarlett Deer?

SCARLETT That's my name, don't wear it out, has to last a lifetime!!

CHRISTINE I'm Christine Pierce from the *Telegraph*. We talked on the phone.

SCARLETT Have a seat.

CHRISTINE Thank you. Nice place.

SCARLETT What, this hole? Sorry if it stinks, I cooked chicken today an ever since I ate it I been fartin up a storm. Dead chicken farts, that's what my brother always said.

CHRISTINE Scarlett, I don't have a lot of time, so is it alright if I ask you some questions?

SCARLETT Sure, How does it feel to be an ugly geek? Fine thank you, fuck you very much.

CHRISTINE Scarlett, advanced cerebral palsy is a serious handicap. Don't you feel that living on your own is dangerous?

SCARLETT Would you like to live in a freakhouse?

CHRISTINE Well, Scarlett, I—

SCARLETT Freedom, freedom girl, I'd rather fuckin rot on the floor of my own home than be well-fed and cared for in a freakhouse.

CHRISTINE What you're saying, then, is that above all things, you cherish freedom. That you would rather risk—

SCARLETT Once when my volunteers were sick? All of em were sick, right? And I just wanted to see what the hell I would do? I lay in my own shit and piss for three days.

CHRISTINE Good Lord, what—

SCARLETT I coulda phoned somebody, my parents live down the street, but I just wanted to see ... I wanted to see how long I'd survive, I wanted to see if I could do it.

CHRISTINE Well, who did you eventually—

SCARLETT My mother, my poor mother. And it makes me sick, sick, because what will I do when they die? They're old you know, they're gonna die soon.

CHRISTINE What will you do?

SCARLETT I'll die on the floor in my shit and piss.

CHRISTINE Scarlett, do you have any hobbies; that is, what do you do between volunteers, do you have favourite soap operas or game shows, or—

SCARLETT I screw my brains out.

CHRISTINE [*a weak laugh*] No, seriously, Scarlett.

SCARLETT You think I'm kiddin? You think I sit around and watch game shows and uh stare out the window waitin for the next volunteer? No way, girlie, I git it ONNN.

CHRISTINE You're ... sexually active, then?

SCARLETT Shocked, aren't you, pretty pea?

CHRISTINE No.

SCARLETT YOU ARE TOO YOU LYING BITCH!!

CHRISTINE Alright, I will admit, I am ... surprised. I suppose the public perception of handicapped people is somewhat—skewered.

SCARLETT You think you're bettern me, dontcha?

CHRISTINE Oh Scarlett, really I ...

SCARLETT Well I'll tell you somethin, Christine, my boyfriend wouldn't rub your tittie. And you think he's handicapped? No way, babe, I'm not fucking a freak.

CHRISTINE Well, I'm very happy for you, really Scarlett.

SCARLETT Bullshit, you think it's sick.

CHRISTINE No, honestly Scarlett, I don't! I think everybody deserves to—have a happy sex life.

SCARLETT Yeah? Wanna hear more?

CHRISTINE Sure!

SCARLETT But don't print this part in your article, right, just the crap about how noble I am copin on my own and that shit, and how good the United Church is helpin me out, all that shit right?

CHRISTINE Scarlett, I won't print anything that you don't want me to. I despise journalists that do that kind of thing. I want you to think of me as a friend. Maybe we could even go out sometime, catch a movie, or go to dinner ...

SCARLETT Sure, if you like.

CHRISTINE So! How did it all start with your boyfriend?

SCARLETT It all started one night, I'd just been watching TV for sixteen hours straight, from eight in the morning, right? And that's hard on the eyes, I was bone tired. So I go to bed, I look out the window and there's no moon, right? And I lie there for hours, can't sleep, itchy, bored, just wishin I was dead, as usual, when I hear, my door open.

CHRISTINE Were you frightened?

SCARLETT I couldnta cared. I thought it was, you know, a guy with a knife, come to carve me up. I thought good, great, whata way to go. I laughed thinkin a Monica, she's my morning volunteer, thinkin a her comin in findin me dead—so I wait to be cut, but I don't hear nothin, nothin, I figure he's in his socks, not a sound then ... he sits on the edge of my bed, and and and, and then he start ... he start ... he start ... touchin my foot just touchin my foot so soft, and nice, and I ... laugh. I laugh and laugh, and Christine, I don't think I ever laughed so long and so long in my life.

CHRISTINE Who was it?

SCARLETT That's the question, isn't it Chris? Who the hell is it?

CHRISTINE Did he ... ever come again?

SCARLETT He come every time there isn't no moon, in like a big cat sit on the bed, and me, like a big piece of fruit,

[*Dance music starts.* SCARLETT *gets up*]

explodin in the heat, exploding up and out the whole night, I can MOVE when my boy comes, [*she twirls*] I am movin, I know I am, I am turnin and swishin and holdin,

[*A* MAN *enters. He and* SCARLETT *dance romantically around the set. He leaves her back in her chair, immobile, and exits*]

like eels, you ever seen eels? Lamprey eels, brilliant light moving fast fast they swim from the Saint John River down to Montego Bay to spurt their young, I swim like that coloured-up, bright and fast when my boy comes, swirlin and movin in the dark no moon ...

CHRISTINE Hey, is he handsome?

SCARLETT I tole you there's no moon.

CHRISTINE You mean you haven't—

SCARLETT He's my midnight man, you dick! My midnight man he is my midnight man, get it? You can't SEE night, you can't SEE when there's no moon why? Why do you think it's so big to see your boyfriend two eyes, nose, a mouth, what the diff, what the hell is the—

CHRISTINE I must go, I ... have an appointment.

SCARLETT You're not gonna print that.

CHRISTINE I have a job, Scarlett, I have a child to support ...

SCARLETT I'll slit your throat if ya print that.

CHRISTINE Goodbye.

[SCARLETT *grabs* CHRISTINE*'s clothing*]

SCARLETT PLEASE!! PLEASE!! Please, Christine, my old lady and old man, they're old, my mum's had a stroke, my dad's got MS, this'd kill em, please!!

CHRISTINE That is not my business, Scarlett, Scarlett, let go of me, LET GO!

SCARLETT Reverend Pete and everybody down the church, they'd think I was a slut, they'd send me to the freakhouse.

[*They struggle*]

CHRISTINE Let me go!!

[SCARLETT *falls on top of* CHRISTINE]

SCARLETT You're gonna kill me, you're gonna kill me.

[CHRISTINE *rolls her off and onto the floor*]

CHRISTINE You are trying to obstruct the freedom of the press, lady.

SCARLETT You can't do this you can't do this!

CHRISTINE [*frees herself, gets away*] I'm sorry. I'm doing it.

SCARLETT I'll see you in hell!!

[*This stops* CHRISTINE]

CHRISTINE What?

SCARLETT I said you'll go right to hell for this!!

CHRISTINE I don't believe in hell.

SCARLETT Joke's on you, girl, cause I'm in it, right now, live from hell, and if you do this, you're gonna be burning here with me, maybe not today, maybe not tomorrow but soon, soon, you'll be whizzing down the highway with a large group of handsome friends to some ski resort or other, and your male driver will decide to pass on the right, you will turn over and over, knocking into each other's skulls breaking each other's necks like eggs in a bag, falling through windshields it's gonna rain blood and I will open my big jaws and swallow youuuu! YOU will spend the rest of eternity inside me. Inside my ... body and ooooh time goes slowwwwwe ...

CHRISTINE You're crazy.

SCARLETT I am waiting for you Chrissy, I'm waiting for you Chrissy, I am waiting for you Chrissy, I am ...

CHRISTINE STOP THAT. Stop that craziness NOW there is no such thing, there is no such thing as any of that ANY of it. You live and you die in your own body and you go up to heaven or just nowhere.

SCARLETT Into the middle of Scarlett ...

CHRISTINE You don't know ANYTHING.

SCARLETT Inside my big wet behind ...

CHRISTINE Stop it. Stop saying those things.

SCARLETT In the bummy of a big dead fish ...

CHRISTINE Stop it, I said stop it now.

SCARLETT Your left arm and your head too, Chrissy, gonna be severed you'll be all over the highway and your mean little soul will ...

CHRISTINE [beats SCARLETT to the ground, screaming] STOP IT! STOP IT! [kicking her] STOP IT! STOP IT! [CHRISTINE collapses]

[SCARLETT breathes with difficulty]

Oh no. Oh no. Scarlett, are you okay? You're okay. You're okay. Your mother will be by soon or a volunteer and, and I'll call, I, I, I'll call an ambulance. You shouldn't have made me do that, Scarlett. You shouldn't have made me kick you like that. The way you, you, you talked to me like that. Like, like, like you belong. In the world. As if you belong. Where did you get that feeling? I want it. I need it. [pause, about to exit] I need it.

SCARLETT OOOOOOH! Come down and kiss me, put your tongue in my mouth!! Come on, NOW, RIGHT now, there's no one around, right now, on the ground, do me, kiss me, come down and kiss me, like a lion, so hot right here right now, swirl, swirl me twirl, twirl me, make me light, light exploding into ... [laughs]

[CHRISTINE *returns, swooping down like a condor, gives* SCARLETT *the kiss of death.* SCARLETT, *thinking it is her lover, responds passionately and then, without air, dies*]

ISOBEL [*to* CHRISTINE, *touching her*] SLAVE! *You* are a slave of the lion! You lie with him you laugh you let him bite your neck, you spread your legs. You will take me to him now.

[*Music, blackout. Lights up on* CHRISTINE's *office. She is moving things in an angry way*]

ISOBEL Shhh. I wait for the lion!!

[RODNEY, *an early-middle-aged man with a stoop,* CHRISTINE's *research assistant, comes in and waits until she addresses him. He has an armload of papers*]

CHRISTINE Yes, Rodney, what is it?
RODNEY I've ... uh ... brought the research material you asked for.
CHRISTINE Good. Great. Thank you ... How was your weekend?
RODNEY Quiet.
CHRISTINE Rodney. Rodney— Rodney I told you I wanted stats on CP, cerebral palsy, not just 'handicapped people.' I wanted information on cerebral palsy!
RODNEY You did NOT specify cerebral palsy, Christine.
CHRISTINE Oh yes I most certainly did, I said—
RODNEY I have it on tape, Christine!
CHRISTINE Rodney! Are you or are you not a professional researcher?
RODNEY Yes.
CHRISTINE Well then start doing professional work! NOW! Or you are out. Is that understood? IS THAT UNDERSTOOD?
RODNEY ... of ... course ...

[CHRISTINE *exits.* RODNEY *is at his desk*]

You will NOT EVER SPEAK TO ME THAT WAY AGAIN CHRISTINE YOU WILL NOT TREAT ME AS AN OBJECT do you understand? Is that understood? IS THAT UNDER-STOOD??

[*Knock on the door*]

Yes? Hello. May I help you?

MICHAEL Yes, I'm looking for a Rodney LeHavre—I was directed to this office.

RODNEY I ... am ... Mr. LeHavre.

MICHAEL Rodney?

RODNEY Do I know you?

MICHAEL Michael ... Lind ... from St. George's, '60 to '64. How are you? You remember me, don't you?

RODNEY Michael ... Lind? No. No, I'm afraid I don't, I'm sorry. Were you in my class?

MICHAEL Yeah, yeah, we were good friends for a while even; don't you remember? Come on. We played chess. You were a great player. You taught me ... how to play. You must remember.

RODNEY Chess.

MICHAEL I guess you don't remember. I'm sorry. I was sure that you'd remember. I ... I ... [backing out]

RODNEY Would you like to come in and sit down? I can take ten minutes I think. Would you like to sit down?

MICHAEL Oh, oh, okay, if you don't mind ...

RODNEY No. A cup of coffee ... I could—get the secretary— Sherry—to—

MICHAEL [laughs] You've got to remember the fly collection. It was really hot. July, I think. We caught it must have been fifty house flies, and, and we stuck them with Elmer's glue, to a piece of Bristol board. To a big piece of Bristol board. And labelled them in Latin. Don't you remember? You must remember.

RODNEY Wait a minute ... wait a minute ... yeah, yeah, and we even *named* them, didn't we? Didn't we name each one?

MICHAEL Yeah, yeah ... I'll never forget. You even named one Clarence. I thought it was brilliant.

RODNEY Right! And yours were all names like Fred, Joe, Cindy, weren't they? Right!

MICHAEL And yours were all royalty—Elizabeth, Margaret, Clarence. God!

RODNEY God. A fly collection. So what did we *do* with it?

MICHAEL I think ... we had it arranged ... to show someone. A colleague of my father's. Someone in insect ...

RODNEY Entomology.

MICHAEL Yeah, that's it. And it was raining or something …

RODNEY Pouring, yes, pouring, and all the flies—

RODNEY & MICHAEL —FELL OFF THE BRISTOL BOARD!

RODNEY God. Michael Lind. Michael LIND! I'm sorry.

CHRISTINE [*off*] Rodney I need that material *as soon as possible,* please!

MICHAEL Well I see that you have to get back to work, I'd better go … Ahhh … just before I go, there's one thing. I uh … this is going to sound strange, but … I've been having … sort of … dreams … about … back then, I … have them a lot—

RODNEY Oh?

MICHAEL Yes, only … I always wake up at the same spot, fairly distressed, actually, and … I just … wondered … if you could … help me … remember … what actually happened. Back then … When we were … kids. Do you think you could—

RODNEY Sure, I could try …

MICHAEL Okay, let's start at the beginning. It was something to do with chess.

RODNEY Chess.

MICHAEL You loved to play chess you … brought me to your house after school, it was a Tuesday, I think, cold, we went through a short cut it said 'Pedestrians Only' I thought it said 'Protestants Only' and I was terrified.

[RODNEY *laughs*]

And we went to your room, with all the paper airplanes hanging from the ceiling all over the room! And we lay on the floor. Do you remember? You remember lying on the floor? Rodney, your carpet. Your carpet was brown and orange, sort of circles or something. There was the sound of a snowblower outside. My queen. You took my queen. And then, and then, Rodney, didn't we laugh, or or or or … some touch some touch Rodney and you made a strange sound. What was that sound. Please help me! I need to go back there. I need to go back there, you see? You were the only—friend that I—we saw the world the same way. Remember? We saw the world the same way. I want to go back there. [*caresses his shoulder*] I want to go back there …

RODNEY I want to go back there, too. I want to go back there, too.

[MICHAEL *and* RODNEY *embrace.* RODNEY *makes the sound.*
MICHAEL *pulls him back and throws him to the ground*]

MICHAEL QUEER!! Queer queer queer queer queer queer QUEER!
FAIRY SISSY LITTLE CREEP!! DON'T YOU EVER ever
remember again. YOU have WRECKED my life, your slimy
memory, using me over and over and over again like an old
porno magazine you will RELINQUISH that memory you will
wipe it out, you understand?

RODNEY You're crazy, you need psychiatric ...

MICHAEL You will NOT remember me again because if you do, if
you do, I will feel it, oh yes, and I will come and I will kill you. I
could feel you remembering, almost daily, I would be in the
middle, the middle of a crucial business meeting all the way in
Vancouver and suddenly I would feel you ... holding my
memory, turning it over and over, folding it, caressing it,
reliving it, SPEWING, spewing your filth all over me. How how
I always wondered how could you do it in the middle of the day?
Did you do it here, at work, at this desk is this where you—

RODNEY Anywhere I can, Michael. You see, my life has been terribly
disappointing.

MICHAEL You will ... free me—

RODNEY Of course. I'll try, but memory ... does seem to have a will
of its own, I can't really help what—

[MICHAEL *hits him, they fight, rolling and punching, and end up on the
floor. Very, very slowly* MICHAEL *raises his head, extends his tongue,*
RODNEY *does the same. They come together and their tongues touch. It
is an ecstatic moment for both of them.* MICHAEL *pulls out a knife,*
RODNEY *takes it from him and cuts his throat.* MICHAEL *dies. Music.
The actor playing* MICHAEL *gets up and exits.* ISOBEL *goes to* RODNEY
and touches him, then RODNEY *gets up, straightens himself*]

RODNEY 'Hello, welcome to St. George's. My name is Rodney
LeHavre, grade seven, and you're ...? Michael Lind! Welcome!
You just came from Vancouver? I have a cousin there! Do you
play chess?' Chess, every day ... chess, Monday, Tuesday,

Wednesday, Thursday, chess, with ... Michael ... at school, at
my house at his house in his room, lying on our stomachs
staring at the chess board, he sticks his tongue out at me because
he had just captured my queen and then I stuck my tongue out
back at him and he moved forward just a bit till his tongue was
touching mine, and my whole life jumped into my tongue we
didn't move just lay there touching tongues, 'Would you boys
like some tuna sandwiches?' his mother the best mother in the
world with her red bangles and bourbon sour at six, 'Okay Mrs.
Lind, thanks!' And we had a secret, an atomic secret nobody else
in the whole entire world knew that we had touched tongues oh
OH wrote his name, MICHAEL, over and over one thousand
times one thousand times; on the fifth day, the fifth day after,
I'm at the blackboard doing math, very good at math, superb
mind for mathematics the other boys jealous, always been
jealous of my superior brain throwing spitballs, used to that,
yelling 'Froggy, froggy frog' because of my francophone name,
used to that, I turn, I catch his face white darkened so quickly
like a sky, he caught, he knew, suddenly he knew, Michael, that
he had been playing chess with the loser 'FROGGY, HEY
FROGGY' they scream 'HEY FROG.' He stands up! They look
expectantly, is the new kid going to defend his friend? What's he
going to say, I to myself, 'Oh thank you, Michael, thank you
thank you the first to ever defend me oh what what are you
going to say to defend me?' He takes a breath, I'm holding mine,
he smiles he speaks he says: 'Is he a frog ... OR A TOAD!!' They
laugh and laugh and laugh screaming their laughter slapping their
desks shaking their fists triumphing a new member of the
PACK!! Is he a frog, or a toad— Am I a frog or am I a toad?

[SHERRY *enters*]

SHERRY RODDEE! RODDEEE!! Baby Bunny.

ISOBEL She!

SHERRY You'll never guess what I have! Milk chocolate bar with lots of
gushy cream in it. Two squares for you, and two squares for me.

ISOBEL She!

SHERRY One hundred and forty calories a square who gives a shit.

I heard Christine chewin ya out, what a fuckin cow.

ISOBEL She ... I see, I smell the spray, the Lion's spray ...

SHERRY [*notices that* RODNEY *is very upset*] What happened?

[SHERRY *runs from* RODNEY'*s office back home to the apartment she shares with her boyfriend of two years,* EDWARD, *an out-of-work actor. When she comes in he is practising a tap routine for an audition. Newspapers all over the floor*]

SHERRY JeSUS I'm peed off—I'm standing on the escalator, right? Goin down to the subway? My back hurts, I don't feel like takin the stairs? So I'm standin there when this woman shoves by me right into the wall and goes, 'Can't *you* move? Some people are in a hurry!' And I just STAND there like a fucking WETWIPE with my mouth open FUCK if I see that bitch again—

EDWARD That's very interesting, Sherry.

SHERRY Whatcha workin on that dance try-out thing?

EDWARD Uh, no. I'm fixing the faulty wiring with my feet, it's magic, Sherry, really! Right through the—

SHERRY Ah Jeez, you're not mad at me again are ya? Whad I do now?

EDWARD I don't know, Sherry, what did you do now?

SHERRY I get off work at five thirty, Ed, it's ten to six what the hell am I supposed to do? Fly home?

EDWARD I phoned work at four o'clock, Sherry, and Arlene said that you had left for the day.

SHERRY Oh well THAT—I was havin a coffee and a piece of cake with Rodney, he—

EDWARD Don't lie, please.

SHERRY I was, Eddie, ask Rodney, ask—

EDWARD You've rehearsed them all.

SHERRY Listen to me! Rodney had some kind of fit today, Christine just about called the cops he was yelling and screaming at nobody all afternoon—he's right nuts.

EDWARD It is a skilful liar it is.

SHERRY *Don't call me 'it'.*

EDWARD I beg your pardon?

SHERRY Have you been drinking? Or doin coke or some shit? You have, haven't you? You—

EDWARD We're out of toilet paper.

SHERRY No, there's more right under the—

EDWARD No there's NOT!

SHERRY Alright, I'll go and get some now—

EDWARD YOU'LL stay right where you are, Sherry. Please. PLEASE I'm asking you. Don't leave me alone—here—I don't want to be alone.

SHERRY Aww Eddie, you know I love you, don't you.

EDWARD If—if you're not happy with my performance in bed … I wish you'd just … tell me and—and—

SHERRY Honey, I love your performance in bed.

EDWARD You don't really, do you?

SHERRY Listen I was just tellin Arlene today you got the best hands of I bet any guy there is on the whole fuckin planet!

EDWARD You were?

SHERRY The way you touch me, Eddie, Christ, I feel like a whole bouquet, you know? A bouquet of red flowers just … poppin open, poppop pop pop pop just like on one of them nature specials. I love makin love with you, I think about it all day, half the time my pants are wet thinkin about you.

EDWARD They're not, really?

SHERRY They are. Feel … feel that [puts his hand under her dress] Oh honey I want you to make love to me. Please?

EDWARD [kissing her] Oh! Oh! I've been thinking about you too, all day, every day.

SHERRY Oh Eddie, I want you.

EDWARD You want me …?

SHERRY Did you not get that part in the TV series? About the runaway kid or whatever? Is that why you're— Eddie what's wrong? Did I say something wrong?

EDWARD YOU ARE A FLAMING ASSHOLE!

SHERRY Eddie!

EDWARD Who are you dreaming about every night?

SHERRY What?

EDWARD Every night you're moaning like an animal in heat, who?

SHERRY What?

EDWARD Who are you dreaming about, Sherry?

Jane Spidell (**SHERRY**) and Julian Richings (**EDWARD**) in the
Tarragon production, November 1990

SHERRY Nobody! I'm not dreaming about—nobody.

EDWARD WHO ARE YOU DREAMING ABOUT?

SHERRY Just forget it, I'm going over to Arlene's I'll see you later.

EDWARD You tell me who you are dreaming about or I will cancel the wedding.

SHERRY Eddie.

EDWARD I will ... TODAY, if you don't stop lying to me treating me like a fucking maggot—

SHERRY I'm not lying to you Ed, please, just—

EDWARD I'll cancel the wedding! I'll phone up Father Hayes and I'll cancel the whole fucking thing.

SHERRY I paid nine hundred dollars for that dress, Eddie.

EDWARD I don't give a flying fuck what you paid for it.

SHERRY EDDIE my mum's got her ticket from Florida, my sisters—

EDWARD I don't give a hot damn miss—

SHERRY OKAY OKAY OKAY OKAY you're right, you're right. There is someone I'm dreaming about; it's ... uh ...

EDWARD It's him, isn't it?

SHERRY Him? Who?

EDWARD The rape from six years ago—

SHERRY [*she throws the telephone book at him*] Eddie THAT is not fair!

EDWARD It's him, isn't it?

SHERRY I think I'm going to be sick!

EDWARD That was the best fuck you ever had, wasn't it? It was the only fuck you ever respected, wasn't it? WASN'T IT, SHERRY?

[SHERRY *cries*]

WASN'T IT? WASN'T IT?

SHERRY NO!

EDWARD Listen to me. You don't tell me the truth right now and I cancel the wedding. RIGHT now, I'll call up Father Hayes and I'll cancel the whole thing for good.

SHERRY Eddie, please!

[*He goes to the phone, flips through the telephone book*]

EDWARD St. Paul's Cathedral, St. Paul's—532—

SHERRY [*she grabs the phone book*] Okay! Okay okay okay!

EDWARD You admit?

[SHERRY *nods*]

What? To what do you admit, Sherry?

SHERRY That ...

EDWARD Come on, tell the truth, the truth, truth, truth.

SHERRY THAT ...

[EDWARD *picks up the phone*]

That he's the best fuck I ever had.

EDWARD NOW we are cooking with GAS. This is what I always knew in my heart never DARED with all this feminist shit going down. Come on, come on tell me if I'm going to be your husband I want to know it all.

SHERRY But what should I—

EDWARD The truth!! I know how hard it is for you after a lifetime of female ... conniving and guile but let's do it! Come on! Tell me, tell me how you led him on.

SHERRY Led ... him ... on??

EDWARD HOW YOU LAID YOUR TRAP! Come on, what was it you were wearing? Wasn't it those sex shorts, those, pink ... what are they called? Sherry, what are they called?

[SHERRY *is saying what she thinks he wants to hear because she is scared, but it is like excrement in her mouth, and* EDWARD *is gratified and ripped apart at the same time by what he hears*]

SHERRY Pink ... hot pants?

EDWARD That's it! And what else, what else?

SHERRY Ahhh ...

EDWARD Come on!

SHERRY No—underwear?

EDWARD Yes? YES?

SHERRY I was a real—cocktease with that guy?

EDWARD Good, good Sherry, the truth is good. And ... AND.

SHERRY Ahh— One—one—time I dropped—dropped my smokes uh—cause I knew the—the sight of my ass in those shorts bending over would make him—him—him—come right in his pants.

EDWARD Yes?

SHERRY See—

EDWARD YES? YES?

SHERRY I—hated—him, I hated him because ...

EDWARD YES?

SHERRY ... because that ... hunger ... I seen when he looked at me
I fuckin hated that ... hunger in his eyes. And his fucking
mouth always open like a fuckin baby bird reachin reachin for
the fuckin worm all the fuckin—

EDWARD So you tortured him!

SHERRY I fuckin hated him—

[*Lines simultaneous:*]

EDWARD Tell me, tell me what happened.

SHERRY Wa—walkin to the subway, about ten o'clock at night,
somethin grabs my arm, it's him, the guy I seen, he asks me if I
want to go to the show, the porno show down the street.

EDWARD You look at him like garbage.

SHERRY I tell him, 'No, asshole.'

EDWARD Like a piece of filth. And?

SHERRY And ... like I told you before, I take off, fast, but—but my
heels are givin me trouble, I can't run in them.

EDWARD You let him catch up.

SHERRY And ... and ... he throws me between two houses, on the
cement, near the trash.

EDWARD Where were all the people, Sherry?

SHERRY I guess they thought we were married, they thought it was
okay.

EDWARD You were very aroused.

SHERRY [*she very obviously was not*] I was ...?

EDWARD And he—pushed you back to the cement?

SHERRY When I tried to get up.

EDWARD And? And?

SHERRY He starts ... smashin my head against the cement!

EDWARD You're so frightened, breathing fast, like an animal!

SHERRY I'm bleeding, and I'm throwing up, and he rips off my
blouse, and my skirt, he—he—he kept telling me that he was

going to kill me.

EDWARD And you're very aroused!

SHERRY He was going to smash my head in and leave me for dead!

EDWARD And then ... he penetrated you?

SHERRY He—he—

EDWARD Inside you?

SHERRY He couldn't get it up, so he used ... he used ...

EDWARD You're moaning with ecstasy.

SHERRY 'I'm gonna kill you, bitch,' he kept sayin, 'I'm gonna kill you, bitch.'

EDWARD The hottest sex you ever had!

SHERRY And ... and ... I lie there for hours, passed out, all my blood pouring out onto the cement.

EDWARD But happy, right? You finally got it GOOD.

SHERRY Until the lady's puttin out her garbage!

EDWARD And you told her the truth, didn't you?

SHERRY What?

EDWARD That it was all your fault.

SHERRY What?

EDWARD That you teased the poor guy, that you wanted him to power you, it was the sexiest hottest sex ever you wanted to be HAD.

SHERRY The lady, she helped me up, she—she gave me a Kleenex, and a glass of water, she—

EDWARD You told her, of course, that you are the snake.

SHERRY I ... am ... the snake?

EDWARD Because SATAN tempts OTHERS to sin, right?

SHERRY Satan tempts others to sin?

EDWARD You were the snake with the diamond back, glittering!

SHERRY I ... am ... the snake.

EDWARD It was all your fault.

SHERRY It was ... all ... my fault.

EDWARD You ARE the snake.

SHERRY I am the snake. I am the snake. I AM the snake. I AM THE SNAKE. I AM THE SNAKE! I AM THE SNAKE! I AM THE SNAKE! I AM THE SNAKE! I AM THE SNAAAAAAAAKE!!

[**SHERRY** *breaks down in tears. She collapses on the floor.*

EDWARD *cleans up and then sits down*]

Eddie? Will you come with me tomorrow then to Ashley's to pick out a pattern? Like I've made the appointment and everything Ed, and after all, you are going to have to live with the dishes. I mean, I know guys hate goin in there, all guys do, but everyone that gets married goes to Ashley's, everyone that gets married—

EDWARD Alright. But nothing with flowers on it. I just want something clean, maybe—white, with a black stripe.

[ISOBEL *enters the room, and offers her hand to* SHERRY, *who takes it, gratefully. Arm in arm, they walk away from* SHERRY *and* EDWARD *'s apartment to a graveyard. At first* ISOBEL *is helping* SHERRY, *but by the time they reach the graveyard, it is* SHERRY *who helps* ISOBEL *find her grave, and gently lays her down, and disappears. In the graveyard, sitting on another tombstone, is* BEN, *the man who killed* ISOBEL *seventeen years before*]

BEN There's one thing, you know. There's one thing that I always ... wanted to tell somebody and that is that ... I done her a favour. I was—kindly—yeah, see, I pull her outa the car and throw her on the cement in front of the warehouse there's a streetlight and ... and she says to me she says, 'Please,' she says, 'Please no strangle, I so ... scared of strangle,' in this voice of breath just ... purely of breath so I stopped, eh? I did. I stepped out of the twister cause that's what it's like, when you're doin something like that, you're inside a twister and to step out, is like ... liftin a dishwasher, eh, but I did. So I go back of the warehouse and I picked up a brick and I hit her—cause she touched me okay? She touched me, right?

[ISOBEL *approaches with her weapon*]

ISOBEL BEN ... ja ... men.

[BEN *looks*]

BEN ja men BEN ja men.
BEN Who the fuck are you?
ISOBEL Is ... o ... bel.
BEN Isobel.

ISOBEL Isobel in July July the one, CANADA day day for CANADA
Birthday. I selling tickets on a Chrysler car, for boys' and girls'
club, one dollar fifty for a ticket. I have five tickets left. I see you
in park. It is raining on park. Don't you remember? I ask you,
'You want to buy ticket on a Chrysler car?' You say, 'Yes, yes, I buy
all five all five tickets. Come into my car, come into my silver
car with dark red meat, come into my car. I will give you the
money for the tickets I have the money in my car,' you said ...

BEN I'm hallucinatin.

ISOBEL I'm Isobel.

BEN You're a picture.

ISOBEL I'm Isobel.

BEN What ... do you want?

ISOBEL I have come.

BEN What do you want?

ISOBEL I am here.

BEN WELL GO AWAY! You hear me? GO AWAY.

ISOBEL [*she is about to kill him with the stick, the forces of vengeance
and forgiveness warring inside her—forgiveness wins*] I love you.

BEN NO!!

ISOBEL *You took my last breath!*

BEN Christ I'm sick, I'm so sick.

ISOBEL *I want back my life. Give me back my life!*

[*Players enter singing a religious-sounding chorale with a sense of
sadness and triumph. They place a veil on* ISOBEL's *head, the actor
playing* BEN *joining them*]

ISOBEL [*an adult now*] I want to tell you now a secret. I was dead, was
killed by lion in long silver car, starving lion, maul maul maul me to
dead, with killing claws over and over my little young face and
chest, over my chest my blood running out he take my heart with.
He take my heart with, in his pocket deep, but my heart talk. Talk
and talk and never be quiet never be quiet. I came back. I take my
life. I want you all to take your life. I want you all to have your life.

[*Players sing a second, joyful chorale, walking off.* ISOBEL *ascends,
in her mind, into heaven. The last thing we see is her veil. End*]

JUDITH THOMPSON was born in 1954 in Montreal, and grew up in Connecticut and Kingston. She received her B.A. from Queen's University and graduated from the acting program of the National Theatre School. *The Crackwalker*, her first play, was a finalist in both the Clifford E. Lee playwrighting competition and the National Repertory Theatre Play Awards, in 1980; *White Biting Dog* won the Governor General's Award for Drama, in 1985; *I Am Yours* won two Dora Awards for acting and a Chalmers Award, in 1987; *Tornado* received a Nelly for Best Radio Drama, in 1988; *The Other Side of the Dark* won the Governor General's Award for Drama, in 1989; and *Lion in the Streets* won a Chalmers Award, in 1991. Judith now lives with her husband and two children in the Annex area of Toronto.

RICHARD PAUL KNOWLES is Chair of the Drama Department, University of Guelph. His introduction draws on material first published in *BRICK* 41 (Summer 1991).

Editor for the Press: Robert Wallace
Cover Design: Gordon Robertson
Cover Illustration: Helen Healy
Production Photographs: Michael Cooper
Printed in Canada

Coach House Press
401 (rear) Huron Street
Toronto, Canada
M5S 2G5